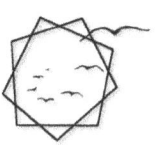

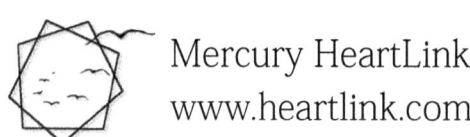

Silver Chain

SILVER CHAIN

poems by Hank Blackwell

Silver Chain: poems

Copyright ©2021 Hank Blackwell

ISBN: 978-1-949652-09-3
Publisher: Mercury HeartLink
Silver City, New Mexico
Printed in the United States of America

Front Cover image: Silver Chain photo by the author
Author photo by author
Drawings for each section: Tim Burns
Cover and layout design: Denise Weaver Ross

All rights reserved. This book, or sections of this book may not be reproduced or transmitted in any form without permission from the author, except for brief quotations embodied in articles, reviews, or used for scholarly purposes.

Permission is granted to educators to create copies of individual poems, with proper credits, for classroom or workshop assignments.

Mercury HeartLink: consult@heartlink.com

Mercury HeartLink
www.heartlink.com

"Poems are like the upwelling of water in the desert. They find their way along some aberrant shear or are wrung from the heart of stone, drop by drop..."

—Chuck Cockelreas

Contents

Why I Cry

Meeting 2
Current 3
Grandchild 4
Noel 5
Long-Lived 6
Breathing 7
Centerpiece 8
Perch 9
Unsung Love Songs 10
The Meaning of Beauty 12
"How Long You Been Farmin'?" 13
Broken Heart 14
Clearly 15
Heroes 16
Father's Odyssey 18

Dark Waters

January Morning 22
Haunted Hotel 23
Dubious Path 24
Frost Line 25
Cobra 26
Great Wall 27
Stray 28
Aeromotor 29
Hiroshima 30
Feeding Hand 31
Hooked 32
Cabin Boy 33
Getting By 34

SUNSET
Old Dog 38
Any Harvest 39
Gettysburg 40
Aisle Seat 41
Antietam 42
Shadow 43
River Stones 44

CROOKED FINGERS
Cowboy Hands 48
Amber Migration 49
Lunar 50
Intersection 52
Cover 53
Higher Self 54
Free 55
Rainbows 56
Recipe 59
Antiphonal 60
Familiar Face 61
Rainbows Revisited 62
Flacon 64
Float 65
Son to Father 66
Sonoran Stroll 67
Carpenter 68
Pale, Yellow Room 69
Oh 70

UNEXPECTED GIFTS

Silver Chain 74
Quiet 75
Tasman 76
Gamelan 77
Wren 78
Bajada 79
Unexpected Visit 80
Blue August Moon 81
Changing Woman 82
Solstice Eve 83
Cottonwoods 84
Arrival 85
Hope 86
Owl 87
Equinox 88
Ancestors 89
Bear 90
Serafina Autumn 91
Avian Wish 92

About the Author

For my daughters who are my heroes.
For my dearest friends...

Acknowledgements

Heartfelt thanks to family and friends, to my Men's Group and others who continue to hold me up and encourage me to be a better human.

Many thanks to Tim Burns and Vittorio La Cerva, wonderful friends who have continuously urged me to share my writing.
Sincere thanks to Vernon Reed, dear friend, artist, and collaborator for over fifty years.

Thanks to Chuck Cockelreas, one of the finest writers and friends on the planet, for his love and encouragement, which never ceases.

Thank you to Pamela Warren Williams, one who not only published this book, but did so with kindness and generosity.

WHY I CRY

Meeting
for my daughters

A first breath,
breaking surface
of glassy lake
somewhere
high in mountain meadow.
Clean, cold air,
perfume
of early summer iris
and columbine

I was changed,
wounds and all.
That instant
rendezvous
with love and fear.
An introduction
to hope...

Current

I resist the urge
to hide beneath grassy ledges
like trout my father would find
in cold streams
that ran through high pastures...
Life sometimes does not move
to confluence.
Instead, it separates
due to the smallest feature
or nudge from gravity.
It is then
that it is best to be the trout,
grateful for the current.

Grandchild

My hand presses on your round belly
anticipating communication...
perhaps a heel, a prenatal high-five.
The humid summer heavy,
reminiscent of my childhood,
I take a first step
back to distant evenings...
returning suddenly to this moment
by the reply
from your daughter's heel.
"Glad to know you, Grandpa",
punctuated
by the neon of a hundred fireflies.
Your homestead,
a father and daughter
plowed like new earth,
mother and grandfather.

NOEL

Last year's journeys
have been upstream
for such a small fry.
Earlier times required
leaping through
backyard sprinklers.
Now, thrust into currents,
forced to swim
to ancient rhythms
usually reserved for elders.

Avoiding net,
hook, talon,
uninvited lessons and scars.
Now wise
and dubious
well beyond your years.
You succeeded.
Strong and wise
now for any journey
Pushing out from eddies
and into current.

Long-Lived

I hold you like a poultice
upon my chest,
breathing in your newborn breath,
warm with innocence.

You dream new dreams,
I am awake with mortality,
already counting days.

May you remember
name, eye color,
the worn threadiness
of a father-voice,
singing lullabies
when there was only us.

Then, take me with you
on visits to your grandchildren.

Breathing

The only sound

in this new house

is the steady rhythm

of your sleeping breaths,

their regularity

breaks like waves

against the empty walls

Centerpiece

You return,
and the missing piece
of the great chalk art puzzle
drawn on an empty driveway
finds its place.
Not at the edges
or at a corner.
It is at the very center.
The color, unfaded
still matching
the piece of chalk
carried every day
since you departed.

Perch

You, very far away,
bird, resting
in snowy piñon,
balanced upon precipice.
Watching.
Unable to reach out
to save you
or break the fall.

Time passes,
tree and perch remain,
further
from my lethargic reach.

Winged hero,
sweet song to sing
strong wing
ready to soar.

Unsung Love Songs

We treat our dreams
as fathers do
their sleeping children —
leaving them quiet and covered,
tending to them silently.

Sleeping there, it is safe
to tell secrets,
sing love songs
unheard.

Waiting late hours,
when kiss and tear fall
upon sleeping cheeks.

Stealing upon our children,
feelings and dreams
whisper the most
sacred parts of ourselves.

Sleeping child will honor
deepest wounds,
most fragile secrets.
The child awake
rewards them.

Homage to night silence,
unable to see wounds,
hear cries,
remaining unaware...

The Meaning of Beauty

missing you
returning
to memories
of brilliance
upon your arrival
beautiful, young woman
changing father's heart
now expert
in gratitude
and knowing
what absolute beauty is...

"How Long You Been Farmin'?"

With bright soul
and steeled will,
you nudge me
into a good garden,
where I must not bolt
across fertile ground
or misuse hoe and spade...
You have shown me light
flowing across furrows
fertile with life's wish.
Sowing patience,
into my own,
seedling soul.
Oh, so sweet,
farming with you.

Broken Heart

No better or worse
than another parent,
despite hopes
and denials.
A father
is often the first
to break a daughter's heart,
the unintended great anchor.

Reprieve takes light
in the beauty
of the gentle, loving men
you have chosen
for yourselves,
and the compassionate paths
you have navigated
on your journeys.

Clearly

Autumn morning
crisp with fattening air,
golden, bright,
as changing leaves.
Southern chevrons breathe,
pointing to winter wheat.
These daughters mark
unique directions.

Life's meaning
cuts clearly with both edges.
The missteps
of a flawed parent.
The gratitude of humble father.
Beautiful,
miraculous children.

Heroes

Heart wants for peace,
sacred space
yearning for love to be my will.
Orbits accelerated,
time is the essence.
Days available
for risk and wonder
now most noticeably fewer.
Old heart,
scarred,
refuses to capitulate.
Wounded, it is wiser
and I, more trusting
of a gentle,
loyal companion.
Beauty found with pain
in candle-lit meeting place.
Miles have worn me,
limitations
an accumulation
of earlier adventures.
Now content to partner
this soul in the choreography
of life's current moments...

Older, finding respite
in honest observation.
No precious time
to disappoint.

Many dark nights,
sorrow and pain
lead to waking,
grateful
for sunrise, birdsong,
embrace of
family and friend.
All failures
lead to here,
the absence of malice
in my shortcomings.

Days of despair and grief
never once separated me
from the heroism
of my children.

Father's Odyssey

I often fear
I may not hold you again
or hear your voice
light upon my heart.
Every embrace remains
as powerful as our first —
father and newborn child.

We fear the worst,
silently hoping for the best...
parenting in absentia
while fears
and gratitude
collaborate
creating a longing
for your presence.

Leap into your adventures!
Fly from the nest,
all the while,
changing the world.
Yet hasten, please,
to come home safely to us.

Dark Waters

January Morning

Sky a clean, deep glacial blue.
Cold, a sharp, steel edge
slicing through
winter breathing.
Stepping cautiously
over driveway ice,
a stroll
away from
solitude.
Quantum physics
of ritual
remain unforgiving,
no gravity between
solitude and isolation.
Crisp steps
upon yesterday's snow,
birdsong and rising sun.
Sadness thaws.
A choice
between gratitude and regret,
isolation and breath,
winter's edge and
the slow, glacial melt.

Haunted Hotel
Jerome, AZ

room ten, upstairs,
paranormal history
a distraction,
luring attention
from the real ghosts
that reside
within a wounded heart.

Dubious Path

unknown fragrance
perfect love
vaulted cathedrals,
weekend retreats.
aroma
seducing judgement,
discipline —
scent inhaled.
potent, invisible,
leading away
from ourselves

Frost Line

ground heaves with
dark winter,
contorting solid, frozen
ice, relentless,
will not retreat,
defies the sun.

stubborn chill,
impudent, nagging
reminder
of line between
frost and thaw,
boundary where
deeds reside
and bide
this cold, gray morning.

Cobra

Perpetually coiled,
tense, ready to strike,
life a startle of threats.
Body and heart
hardened and flexed,
ready for the next hand
to envenomate.

Great Wall

History whispers quiet words,
delivers hints
not to be trusted.
Sentiment more audible
than vocabulary,
intuition powerful
and dangerous.
Years in translation.

Failures
missteps...
the great wall
of disappointment.

Time
seasons parting,
easing pains
that have festered
on both sides of boundary.

Stray

I hesitate
to accept the promises
of other wounded souls.
Without them,
I live like a stray dog
hoping for food,
expecting the boot,
hungry, bruised,
burying rotting dreams
deep within damp soil
and will not turn them
up to dry
in someone else's sun.

Aeromotor

For the eldest
it is over now.
Decades of revolutions
from sibling windmills.
Rusted, old,
distorted from multitudes
of gale and thunderstorm.
No hub needed now
To hold vane and blade.
Each must weather wind
and revolution independently.

Hiroshima

Ground
and monument
(re-planted, cleansed)
contains
birdsong and laughter
amidst dark relics.
Yet unable
to mask suffering cries
of burned masses
or
deafening crack
and release
of blinding, white light
and heat
of so many suns.
New, re-born city,
Grass and fountain,
invisible souls,
now shadows
upon granite canvasses.

Feeding Hand

Mangled.
Dried blood caked
over torn flesh,
broken bone.
Time
will reveal
knitting
or necrosis.
The feeding hand-
bitten, chewed,
spat out.
Secrets...

Hooked

struggling to undo
the line of dreams
tied to the hook.
taut line pulls
toward shallows
broiling, desperate
pulling against rod and reel,
toward open water.

I cannot follow
where you go,
only slip in and out
of shadowy currents,
toward deeper waters.

Cabin Boy

Gales and high seas
have nearly drowned me.
This ship, battered,
remains afloat.
It did not ground
or break apart
upon hidden reef.
Buffeted upon albatross wind,
sails full.
Moorings and capstan
tear at callouses,
tides pull seaward
toward the adventure...

Getting By

Like the calloused farmer
on the long road,
growing the same crops,
wearing the same, muddy boots,
I got by.
Like the old dog,
circling the same pillow,
barking the same warning,
chasing the same tail,
I got by.
Like the lonely bachelor,
voicing the same complaints,
hiding in the same shadows,
crying the same, lonely tears,
I got by.
Farmer tried to plow you under,
dog, defending pillow,
bared teeth.
Lonely man turned saboteur.

You remained, determined,
not letting me by.

Sunset

Old Dog

Graying muzzle,
slow to rise
with the weight
of many runs
and skirmishes.
Growls at
those who would
scratch scarred ears,
escapes through open gates,
away from warm meals,
loving company.
Barking at neighbors,
chewing shoes and
chair legs.

You remain,
unconditional, patient
dear friend.
Old dog returns,
gratefully circling
the worn pillow
at your feet.

Any Harvest

Beneath hat,
shaded from
piercing summer sun,
walking remote hills.
Dust rises beneath footsteps
over dry mounds.
Gray cheatgrass
waiting for rain.
This moment I am all there is,
mixed blessing.
Freedom
fills one pocket.
The other remains empty.
Repairing, coaxing
baked earth
and self
not to die.
waiting, patiently...

Gettysburg

Open fields, boulders,
evening wind...
setting sun cut up
by stands of trees
where
so many fell.
Here,
last moment of safety
before the charge.
Wounded, dying now lay twisted.
Cannonade and gunpowder gone.
Soaring birds
bring souls down to roost
upon monument and ridge.
Deer begin to walk,
stepping lightly
on hallowed ground.
Shadows grow
among these places
in the absent thunder
of a hundred cannons.

Aisle Seat

Pale hand rests
upon airline magazine,
that is all
I can see of her.
Maybe from Texas,
nails so perfect.
It cannot tell stories,
does not wave
or caress
as others
that I have held.

Antietam

Fall chevrons mark seasons
above wheatfield stubble.
Here, among ripening grain
and peach,
shot like hungry robins
falling in obtuse piles
filling the bloody lane.
Charging through cornfield rows
toward the fences
where they all fell.

Shadow

My shadow grows longer,
walks slow.
I take note
of the intention
of my gait,
sun on my back
breaking over tired shoulders
like rippled water.
My shadow lengthens,
telegraphing sunset,
the final glorious reflection
of my waning light.
Wispy memories
against spacious sky.
My shadow grows longer.
Content, I marvel
as it stretches
and weakens,
still dutifully connected
to these last journeys.

River Stones

Each moment begins.
Sharp stone,
fractured from the vein
falling into swift current
of life's river.
One after another,
tumbling
over soft silt
and hardened boulder,
surfaces beginning to polish.
Rounded and smooth,
soon similar
in size and weight.
Finally, arriving home.
Tiny, glittering grains
upon the endless beach.

CROOKED FINGERS

Cowboy Hands

The wounds have
knit together, slowly
the rough edges of the tear,
tattered blanket ends,
searching for an even line.
Dagger wounds, deep,
heal more readily,
cleaner edges.
Ripped fabric
leaves uneven scars,
sore to the touch,
distorted.
Deeper, irregular,
layered over others.
A knotty gauze
tying chapters together.
Old cowboy hands,
maps of paths
travelled and not taken.
Unseen, amidst the scars
remains a grateful and loving heart.

Amber Migration

winged presence silently passes
skyward
casting feathery
shadows where I long to follow
a reminder:
one departs,
another stays

I remain
grounded, watching you,
ascending to migrate
in search of another chevron.

amber fragrance dissipates
with your departure—
it was
the only perfume
I had learned
to trust.

Lunar

Moon is down, emeralds gone
will you be found
when night is done?

Stage is dark,
curtain down
heart feels haunted
not a ghost in town.

Moon is down, emeralds gone
will you be found
when night is done?

Long hours
before rising sun
wake or dream
lost or won?

Moon is down, emeralds gone
will you be found
when night is done?

Love may dim
in evening sky
slowly fading,
not truth, not lie.

Moon is down, emeralds gone
will you be found
when night is done?

Love, a twin
never faded
through crooked years,
times elated.

Moon is down, emeralds gone
will you be found
when night is done?

INTERSECTION

I have wandered off the path again,
distracted by trees and wildflowers.
Lost, anxious, I search for the way home.
Pushing against panic,
not to bolt in a wrong direction.
I breathe and wait,
hoping my path will be found
and intersect with yours.

Cover

every hat has a story
punctuated by squinted eye.
the old, stained brim,
reminder of times gone by.

every hat has purpose,
a statement on our head,
cover and symbol
of words that must be said.

this hat holds feelings
from time ago when we met
now, a reminder.
Things may happen yet...

Higher Self

Fresh baked bread,
piñon smoke...
summer storm
thunder
rolling over wet sandstone,
growing resonance
of canyon wren's call:
nature's Beethoven,
invisible.
Laughter
and gentle, sleeping breaths.
Sacred, thousand - year embrace,
always
inside of you.

FREE

It is done.
Like an overweight astronaut
defying gravity
leaving reassuring anchor,
rocketing upward,
creating
distance.
History shrinks below;
the exhilaration
of weightlessness arrives.

Rainbows

Wherever you go.
However far away it is.
Take my love
   on your shoulders, riding
                       as I did
down those steep trails to our fishing place.
(The only time I remember embracing you
      as a child)
Smelling the cigarette smoke, the sweat
      the canvas vest
           like perfume,
    the smell of a father
               to a son.
Wherever you go,
     cast away your silent desperation
    like a dry fly into the current.

I will probably walk those trails
                When you are gone...
     crying, remembering how you were
          during those magical times.

I felt your body move as it carried me
                         down to the river.
        You in search of trout.
                Me, hoping the trail
                              would never end.
You will die a stranger to me.
        Unable to attend to my desires
                             as a son,
        I wished you could be as gentle with me
                as you were
        when tying a fisherman's knot to the hook.

Perhaps I don't go fishing now because I fear
          the intrusion of those trips we made or
          confusing fragmented memories of them...

Only the two of us
          down that steep rocky trail
                         into the gorge.

You, fishing for trout,
                          me, for you.

I hoped you would look my way
                and leave the rod,
                  the line and the little fly,
      and reel me in.

When you go even as a stranger,
      I will always hold those few trips
            like rainbows, in my little creel,
      and I will remember you
             carrying me down that trail...

Recipe

New years, new days,
passing hours, minutes,
cups of flour,
teaspoons of salt,
pinches of herbs.
How much,
how long,
how enough.
Might hours and days
be moments?
Could tons, pounds
and tablespoons
become just what is needed?

Antiphonal

Not able to be passionate
with words or embraces,
finally lured out
by life's energy...
Hesitation sings
to a stone
surrounded by currents
of fear...
Song whispers,
barely heard
above the rushing water.
Wavering between the antiphonal,
glancing
between horizon and stone.
Cautioned in whispers,
fearful of betrayal
by reluctance.

Familiar Face

My father sleeps fitfully,
White whiskers shading his pain.
I am not ready for his face.
I have not yet earned it ...

Rainbows Revisited
Big Arsenic Springs, Rio Grande Gorge, NM

Six decades; sixty orbits
when I last traveled
this rocky cathedral trail,
where you found peace
and I, you.
Retracing old footsteps,
childhood aromas
toward the river below.
Spring gurgles from sawgrass,
pours itself into
muddy eddies.
Mother Rio.
A promise,
carrying you down that trail
as you
had once carried me
so many years before.
Trout still rising in pools
where you had taught me
they would be waiting,
water, cold, present, reliable
graceful down canyon serpentine.

Ashes course down tiny spring
into mighty river.
This promise
another loving gift,
from you to me.

Flacon

this
undoing
my doing;
this doing,
my
undoing.
this dying,
my undying,
this undying
my dying.
this bleeding,
my healing;
this healing,
my slow bleeding.
this aging vessel, now
a container for the perfume
of fragrant passing of memories

Float

One memento each.
From father
and his.
Bamboo fly rod
arc and catapult
century-old hopes,
gently upon pearl river.
Cane and leather creel:
father's
fishing costume.
Father and son,
long done,
connected in
trout-hope.

Son to Father

Paternal assumption,
supporting the family,
oldest son
strong and stoic.
Loving words offered to Mother,
brother, sister, grandchildren.
Your passing reflected
with friends, neighbors.

Assembling
this broken family,
awaiting permissions
for last breath,
son's assurances
whispered.

Death lays you thin and still
beneath your portrait.
Hands no longer touch,
smile now open gape.
I cannot indulge,
nor consult,
your voice forever gone.

Sonoran Stroll

Fine, red caliche
records boot prints
perhaps to be discovered
in twenty centuries.
Amidst cryptogam,
juniper,
coyote signs,
knapped flint,
faint sounds from ancients.
Higher
toward mesa feet,
shadowy topography.
Savannah cuneiform
waiting to be read.

CARPENTER

I wonder when you will arrive.
On the coldest evening.
Alone,
battered Toyota your sleigh,
delivering ornaments
from elf-less workshop.
Christmas carpenter,
no donkey or virgin...
This inn, always open
for ornament
and you.
Wise man, just outside the circle,
gift hung upon the tree.

Unexpected Gifts

Silver Chain

My life,
a silver chain
connecting
one chapter
to another.
It holds heavy
the number
of loved ones
that hang brightly
from its tarnished links...

Quiet

everything hunts
in early autumn light
quail for gravel,
swallows for insects
with heavy wet wings
flickers drill for
meals hiding below bark
brook sings
to meadow
wind weaving tall grass

Tasman

Unseen currents flow
urged by lunar pull
filling crescent bay,
abundant rendezvous.
Boundaries intertwine,
ancestors mingle in
rhythms most ancient.

Gamelan

Morning light called.
Raucous paddy prayers.
Frogs flirting,
ducks impatient.
Crickets cracking comb-legs.
Songbirds waking.
Ancestors walk,
blessing the fields.

Wren

Staccato welcome
echoes up canyons,
varnished sandstone,
ancient river-wood
now stone.
Waking ancients,
racing raven down canyon
to fertile
cholla and scallion deltas.
Centuries move on.
Your song remains,
leading
to sacred places
worshipped many songs ago...

Bajada

Headlights wink dimly
through morning fog
beneath a fuzzy harvest moon.
Piñon become buffalo
grazing on century old grass.
Clouds stoop lower,
pushing back dawn.
Eagles begin morning hunts.
Resting occasionally upon
old cottonwoods
that scattered moonlight
generations ago.

Unexpected Visit

a dozen days
since haunting
owl voices
beckoned,
year-long
coma of sadness
ended.

now, able to notice
healing scars
on wounded heart,
released by pointed talons

long-awaited breath
now filling
once starving lungs,
feeding fresh hope
to every hungry space,
no longer dying....

Blue August Moon

leaning in
with magic light.
Illuminating living river
bleeding red this sacred night.
Once calm and muddy
with rain the serpent's grown
changing liquid skin to red
soon after the ring was thrown.
May moon and river take it,
decoration worn.
Wipe it clean and bury it
with the pain from which it's borne.
Blue moon, red river
joined in night's reflection
Blue moon, red river,
cycle of perfection...

Changing Woman

Do you know what is under that pinecone?

The world, my son.
        The earth, my daughter.

Do you know what is under that stone?

The world, my daughter.
        The earth, my son.

Your Mother!
Cradling that pinecone,
enduring the weight of that stone,

As gently
as the soles of your feet.

Solstice Eve

Quiet arrives elegantly,
wings spread into stall,
alighting upon branch
beneath low winter sun.
A gift arrives,
single snowflake
settling...

Cottonwoods

Their whispers
fall upon eyelashes, chest
and folded arms.
Wet from the lake,
lying alone with grateful breath,
and opened eyes.
Hundreds
lifting up pain.
Angels answering,
gently lifting fears,
misgivings.
Mistrust dissipated
among gentle summer updrafts.
Spirals,
revealing presence,
gently calming the space
between the "I's"

Arrival

Thunder looms north.
Clouds roil and drop,
heavy with monsoon rain.
Last acres of sunlight
warm mossy earth,
cast long shadows
among twisted fir.
Broken shadows
land hard.
Quiet blows downslope
here.

Hope

ground softened
from summer rain
thunder grumbles
behind ridges
ponderosa
swaying with monsoon wind
long needles wet
with welcomed water
safe serene sacred
elder waits
branches open high above the duff
patiently.
vanilla and wisdom,
relatives embrace.

Owl
03.29.2016, 5:03 a.m., Tesuque, NM

Owls' gentle calls
ended dreaming.
Soft, calming notes
float through spring morning
between sleep and awake.
Measured to the minute,
one exact orbit.

Songs of finch, jay,
raven, junco, and towhee,
yet never owl.
Grateful for mysteries
delivered
upon synchronous wing.

Equinox

Autumn morning,
sun low,
reflecting breath.
Birds try on
winter feathers,
in dressing room chamisa.
Time returns
to gather
migration,
harvest,
retreat below ground.
Life prepares for
the simple,
planetary nod.

Ancestors

Every autumn life migrates,
changes location;
a law, irrefutable.
Planet changes its nod to the sun
chrysalis morning light
emerges with new wings.
Stirrings arise.
We gaze skyward,
life urging each cell.

Hue, scent, frost...
ancient tongues
cranes, singing,
soar above us.

Bear

Knowing our slow move
toward slumber,
startled us with
confident cadence.
Turned head
and steady gaze,
drawing us away
from the hypnosis
of evening campfire,
the very moment of autumn
 illuminated upon her back.

Serafina Autumn

Morning clouds loom low,
(remnants of passing rain)
nestling in the mesas
like kittens.
Belated storm calmed
desert nerves,
cool morning
and wet earth
coaxing shelved hope
back into focus.
Purple asters opened.

Avian Wish

the bird sings,
our ear turns ever so slightly,
our hearts flutter in approval,
unaware of the importance
of every note of every song
to every bird,
each note, a prayer.

About the Author

Born in New Mexico, Hank also lived in Mexico and Texas. He has been a teacher since his early teens, a jeweler, ballet dancer, mountaineer, writer, fire chief and emergency medical services and technical rescue professional. He has travelled extensively and is an avid outdoorsman, athlete, and volunteer. These diverse and varied opportunities such as observation, gratitude, wonder, emotion, and vulnerability created a diverse recipe for the importance of poetry in Hank's life.

Hank grew up in the fifties and sixties, earning his bachelor's degrees in English and Sociology at the University of Texas/Austin, and his master's in Public Administration at UNM/Albuquerque. His experiences in other countries, consulting, participating in the arts, teaching and as a first responder at the local, state, and national levels have all deeply influenced his poetry and world views. The gifts of observing and being fully in nature, humanity and creativity have offered him a unique perspective as a writer. Hank's love of poetry and the breadth of his writing have always been influenced by these varied experiences as well as the extraordinary company of his dear friends. He has been writing for almost fifty years and is the author of *Halfway, a Collection of Thoughts* (Tyler Press, Austin, TX 1977). His poetry has appeared over the years in numerous publications.

Hank is most proud of his three incredible daughters. Their strength, compassion, generosity, and kindness have always been his motivation and joy. Hank now enjoys retirement where he lives in Northern New Mexico.

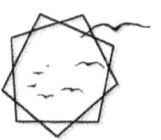

www.ingramcontent.com/pod-product-compliance
Lightning Source LLC
Chambersburg PA
CBHW030812090426

42736CB00028B/1267